AFRICAN AMERICAN HISTORY & DEVOTIONS

Readings and Activities for Individuals,
Families, and Communities

Foreword by Sharma D. Lewis
Teresa L. Fry Brown

Abingdon Press | Nashville

AFRICAN AMERICAN HISTORY & DEVOTIONS:
READINGS AND ACTIVITIES FOR INDIVIDUALS, FAMILIES, AND COMMUNITIES

This book is printed on acid-free, recycled paper.
ISBN 978-1-5018-4955-8
e-pub 978-1-5018-4956-5

18 19 20 21 22 23 24 25 26 27—10 9 8 7 6 5 4 3 2 1
MANUFACTURED IN THE UNITED STATES OF AMERICA

Contents

A NOTE ABOUT ACTIVITIES:

Each reading is accompanied by three activities: one to *do*, one to *discuss*, and one to *dig deeper*. The first activity is meant to be quick but poignant, low-prep, and interactive. The questions for discussion can be thought of as questions to consider if working through the book as an individual. The third activity requires a greater investment of time and resources as you *dig deeper* into the topic. Pick a few of these to try throughout your reading!

Foreword

I first met Dr. Teresa Fry Brown when she was one of the guest preachers for the first Women's Conference at Ben Hill United Methodist Church, in Atlanta, Georgia that my ministry team coordinated. I remember her being eloquently introduced with numerous achievements and accolades. She approached the pulpit and politely removed her shoes, saying, "Sisters, before I preach, I must remove my shoes because we are standing on holy ground." From that day forward I've listened, watched, and admired her vivid illustrations, exegetical research, and powerful delivery of sermons that come alive within your soul!

Once again, her love for storytelling, the rich history of African American culture, and the embodiment of the gospel message have been demonstrated in this literary work. Dr. Fry Brown reminds us in this edition of *African American History and Devotions* that African Americans have shaped civil rights, music, law, medicine, education, politics, theater, and religion in the culture in which we live. We stand on the shoulders of our mothers, fathers, brothers, and sisters who have blazed the trail before us. This collection of daily devotions highlights known and unknown people, organizations, and events that have made contributions in shaping African American culture. She has uniquely crafted the devotions using scripture, meditations, sentence prayers, and activities to tell and explore our story.

There are many gems and insights in this book. Read it carefully with your youth to expose them to our all-too-often-unknown history. Celebrate the milestones of struggles we have overcome as people of African descent. Use it in your Bible studies and churches for "Black History Moments." As always, I am grateful for this gift of words from Dr. Fry Brown.

Sharma D. Lewis
Resident Bishop Richmond Episcopal Area
The United Methodist Church

African American History & Devotions

These Are They

Then he said to me, "These people have come out of great hardship.
They have washed their robes and made them white in the Lamb's blood.
—Revelation 7:14b

Read Revelation 7:13–17

Lying back to front, shackled neck and foot, inhaling odors of decaying flesh and salty tears, hearing groans of captive humanity, gazing into darkness and seeing reflections of hopelessness for 3,700 miles would cause most human beings to focus only on the end of time. During 350 years of fifty-four thousand transatlantic slave voyages, lasting five to twelve weeks each, twelve million North African men, women, and children from many nations floated in terror in the midst of a great crucible called the Middle Passage. Approximately two million died from starvation, malnutrition, murder, and mutiny. Millions of survivors were traded for tobacco, molasses, animals, and cheap labor in North America, South America, and the Caribbean in open-air markets, stripped of the last vestige of their humanity.

An imprisoned John, the writer of Revelation, describes another Middle Passage for seven churches in Asia Minor—Ephesus, Smyrna, Pergamum, Thyatira, Sardis, Philadelphia, and Laodicea. John speaks of the promise of ultimate deliverance from persecution to everyone who believes in God regardless of their situation. The faithful will endure accusations, humiliation, beatings, famine, disease, and even death as they await the promise of eternal life. After these catastrophic events, God's promise is that those from every nation will receive a cleansing, healing bath in the blood of Jesus and will never again endure hunger, thirst, heat, or tears. The slavery of sin will be vanquished. All will be welcomed before God's throne of protection. All will worship God regardless of what they have endured.

The Middle Passage of many enslaved Africans ended generations later as sons and daughters became doctors, inventors, teachers, politicians, athletes, entertainers, preachers, and astronauts. The resiliency and character of survivors of the nightmare slavery enabled hope to shine through the darkness of the ships' hulls as they waited on the move of God.

Prayer: Lord of all, enable us to persevere when we do not understand why we are going through situations or when difficulties will end. Amen.

Do: Have participants side by side, head to foot, as close as possible, for about ten minutes on a bare floor, not moving, without laughter or talking. Discuss how it feels to be so confined and imagine how long you would be able to remain in that position.

Discuss: How do you define resiliency? Where do you see it in our world today?

Dig Deeper: Read Lest We Forget: The Passage from Africa to Slavery and Emancipation, *a three-dimensional interactive book by Velma Maia Thomas containing photographs and documents. Consider the impact the lives lost in the Middle Passage could have had on the world. How do we remember and honor them today?*

Even If

But if he doesn't, know this for certain, Your Majesty:
we will never serve your gods or worship the gold statue you've set up."
—Daniel 3:18

Read Daniel 3:1–30

Hananiah, Azariah, and Mishael were young, handsome Israelite nobility who were taken into service in King Nebuchadnezzar's court in Babylon during a period of captivity. Their names were changed to Shadrach, Meshach, and Abednego. They, along with their friend Daniel, were stripped of their language, names, families, and identities. They were taught the customs and habits of the Babylonians. Assimilation was the order of the day. But they refused to eat the palace food and ate only vegetables and drank water. They held onto their beliefs and would not violate their dietary rules. They thrived. They were the best and the brightest of all the persons in the kingdom. They were eventually placed in leadership positions over the province of Babylon.

The difficulty arose when the king constructed an enormous golden image of himself and decreed that everyone in the nation should worship it. Hananiah, Mishael, and Azariah refused to bow down and were sentenced to death by burning in the royal furnace. They told the king that even if God did not save them, they would still believe in their God.

This type of faith was demonstrated by the black worshipers at St. George's Methodist Episcopal Church in Philadelphia in 1787. Although freed Blacks worshiped at 5:30 each Sunday, contributed the bulk of the offerings, and constructed even the balconies they worshiped in, during the "regular" service they were not allowed to take communion with the white congregants. In August 1794 Richard Allen, Absalom Jones, and eight other men and women attempted to pray at the altar during the worship service and were forcibly removed by a church officer. They rose, walked out of St. George's, and began the Free Africa Society, which led to the establishment of the African Church of Philadelphia. This group eventually split into the Allen-led Bethel African Methodist Episcopal Church (AME) and the Jones-led St. Thomas African Episcopal Church.

Prayer: God of grace and God of glory, help us to continue to have faith in you and to believe even if others do not believe. Amen.

Do: Daniel's friends were renamed by their oppressors. Assign group members new names. For the rest of the session, call one another by their new names. If you are not in a group, write a one-paragraph biography about yourself using your new name. Did you like your assigned name? How did it feel to be called someone you're not? In what ways did it affect your sense of personal power?

Discuss: What does it mean to worship "a God of equal access"?

Dig Deeper: Visit family cemeteries. Share memories of and give libations or honor to your ancestors and share with one another how their lives continue in you.

An Act of Resistance

*Now the two midwives respected God so they didn't obey
the Egyptian king's order. Instead, they let the baby boys live.*
—Exodus 1:17

Read Exodus 1:8–21

Harriet Tubman, Eliza Ann Gardner, William Still, and the other Underground Railroad workers of the nineteenth century were not sociologists with current statistics on population transitions. They were not engineers or explorers with precise instruments predicting how long the road would be or what direction along their journey would be the least difficult or dangerous. Shiphrah and Puah and the other Hebrew midwives knew when to be present with mothers during labor on the birthing stools. They understood breathing, pushing and pulling, and pain. They knew how to catch the babies before they hit the ground, and how to clean them after birth. They helped the babies breathe in their initial breath of life outside the womb. They even knew how to name the child and to teach the mother how to nurture. They were not gynecologists, engineers, or sociologists; but they knew that they had a duty, an obligation to save lives. Shiphrah and Puah defied the pharaoh and refused to kill the baby boys. They lied and said that the Hebrew women were so vigorous during birth that they did not have time to be present when boys were born. They feared God more than the king.

The "conductors" of the freedom train or Underground Railroad, a network of barns, churches, houses, boats, carts, wagons, trains, and footpaths, used any means necessary to assist between forty thousand

and one hundred thousand runaway enslaved persons to freedom in the North and Canada. Some were shipped in boxes like Henry "Box" Brown who mailed himself to Philadelphia. Others passed for white disguised as aristocrats. All defied the orders of the master/kings and let the boys and girls, men and women live. Like Shiphrah and Puah they risked their lives to save someone else. God rewarded the midwives' courage with homes and families of their own. God rewarded the surviving courageous conductors with knowledge that they helped somebody breathe freedom.

Prayer: God, give us courage to help somebody even as we risk our own comfort. Amen.

Do: Draw a courage map of your life. When have you had to be most courageous? How did you do it?

Discuss: What would you do to keep others safe? If you have limits, what are they?

Dig Deeper: The Underground Railroad was multiethnic, ecumenical, and spanned ages and economic status. Challenge each person to find seven locations or stops of the Underground Railroad and five persons (other than Harriet Tubman) who participated. What were their motivations?

Look in the Mirror

God created humanity in God's own image,
in the divine image God created them,
male and female God created them.
—*Genesis 1:27*

Read Genesis 1:26–28

"God is a Negro" was preached often by Bishop Henry McNeal Turner, startling Black Methodist and Baptist congregations in the nineteenth century. Turner was an African Methodist Episcopal (AME) Church leader, Reconstruction-era Georgia politician, a staunch defender of the Civil Rights Act of 1875, an outspoken defender of African American rights, prominent leader of the 1870s back-to-Africa and Haiti movements, and supporter of the American Colonization Society. He served briefly as postmaster in Macon, Georgia, and in 1870 was again elected to the state legislature. He ordained Sarah Hughes in 1884, going against the pattern established in the AME Church, and was reprimanded. He worked with President Lincoln to establish the first black regiment in the Civil War and served as the first black chaplain in the military.

An advocate of Black pride, Bishop Turner argued that Blacks should reject any and all teachings by Whites that Blacks were inferior. He said that black people needed to reflect on their identity as people who were made in God's image, therefore God was Black. He believed the Genesis account of God's creative purpose. God created Adam and Eve, male and female, in God's image. We were conceived as mirror images of God, to think about God, to love like God, to act by God's direction.

Turner wrote, preached, and taught that each person, particularly each Black person, looks like God. We are each handmade, God-breathed, earthen miniatures of God—short, tall, young, older, full-figured, thin-figured, athletic, disabled, Black, White, Brown, Red, Yellow—just like God. In a world where people evaluated the worth of others by skin color, Turner was a voice crying in the wilderness. His controversial statements influenced his popularity and eventually undermined his move toward national leadership, but he never backed down.

Prayer: Creator God, we are grateful you fashioned us just as you wanted us to be, wonderfully, marvelously produced sons and daughters. Amen

Do: Draw a picture of God. It can be as abstract or literal as you want. What does it mean for us to be made in God's image?

Discuss: Can you draw parallels between Bishop Turner and any African American public figures today? If so, who? How are they alike? How are they different?

Dig Deeper: Using your collective knowledge and oral history, construct a family genealogy covering as many generations as possible. How far back can you go without consulting other resources?

No Need to Beg

I will put my breath in you, and you will live.
I will plant you on your fertile land.
—Ezekiel 37:14a

Read Ezekiel 37:1–14

Ezekiel 37 is one of the classic texts preached in Black churches. By the power of the Holy Spirit the Old Testament prophet Ezekiel relays a message to the faithful remnant of God's people, sanctifying and replenishing authority years after the fall of disobedient Israel. In the vision the remnant of Israel is forced to walk miles into captivity and death in the valley of the Tigris and Euphrates. The rich imagery of God's Spirit reconstructing bone fragments in anatomical order, foot to head, is captivating. The ground of hope is that God can take nothing and make it something. God will make life appear in death-defined situations. God is able to infuse even the direst situations with new opportunities. God sends the four winds of the Spirit to activate the bodies representing Israel's demise. God opens graves of despair, disappointment, and disenfranchisement with a promise to bring the disenfranchised back to their land. God, and God alone, will supply each person with his or her own soil, own place in this world.

The settlers and founders of Black townships must have understood what Billie Holiday would sing years later "God bless the child that's got his own." God gave them their own soil as they set out to establish cities where they could experience the dignity of their personhood. There were hundreds of Black townships established between the late sixteenth and early twentieth centuries. Many were destroyed by militant Whites, dwindled by economic downturns, or suffered limited sustainability due to insufficient planning. The first, for free Blacks who converted to Catholicism, was established in 1562 just outside St. Augustine, Florida. Princeville, North Carolina, was established in 1865 by the formerly enslaved after the Civil War. It was the first independently governed Black community. Joseph Clark purchased 112 acres of land from Josiah Eaton in 1887, and Eatonville became the first incorporated Black municipality in America. God provided the space and fulfilled the promise for their faithfulness.

Prayer: Help us, God our Provider, to receive your promise of a place in this life, which no one can take away. Amen.

Do: Listen to or read the lyrics of Billy Holiday's "God Bless the Child." Would you say you've "got your own"? Why or why not?

Discuss: Describe what you think Ezekiel saw when the dry bones came alive. Now describe what that might look like in someone's life today. Share examples you have seen of new life coming to dry bones.

Dig Deeper: Explore the history of the first Black church in your city. Explore deeds or public records, news clippings, obituaries, websites, or interviews with members to find out as much as you can about its history and current status.

Pass It On

One generation will praise your works to the next one,
    proclaiming your mighty acts.
—Psalm 145:4

Read Psalm 145

It has been said that music is the universal equalizer. Each culture has a body of music that defines who they are, distinguishes what they believe, delineates their sense of beauty, and may determine how they pass their experiences on to the next generation. The corpus of music known as Negro Spirituals is unique to the Black experience in America. It includes themes of escape modalities, protest against oppression, human relationships, God's promises, the life and death of Jesus, eternal life, and earthly freedom.

Psalm 145 is part of a corpus of music sung by ancient people of faith with themes similar to those in the spirituals. God's mercy, grace, greatness, works, faithfulness, glory, and acts are to be proclaimed forever and ever. Each person has a duty to tell someone else about what God has already done and what God will do. God's acts and actions do not change. Every generation is required to teach the succeeding one about God. Music is one way of teaching and expressing.

The Fisk Jubilee Singers, beginning in 1871, launched a worldwide tour lauding God's works in song. Abolitionist and music lover George White and nine students traveled the North and made three tours of Europe garnering $150,000, a significant amount even by today's standards. Some were hesitant to share the music of their ancestors, but it was well received. Standards included "Steal Away," "Ain't Got Time to

Die," "Swing Low, Sweet Chariot," and "This Little Light of Mine." They encountered all types of prejudice and personal difficulty. What started as a fundraiser for the school became a diplomatic means of teaching often-forgotten spirituals to an international audience. The spirituals were a way to keep the relationship between God and enslaved persons alive.

Prayer: Lord, put a song in our hearts and on our lips so that we can tell others about who you are and whose we are. Amen.

Do: What are your favorite spirituals? Pick one to sing.

Discuss: Who taught you the songs of faith? What's your earliest memory of singing the faith?

Dig Deeper: Have a young person interview an elder, at least twenty years older. Ask questions about their childhood, family, hopes, regrets, and dreams. Video the interview. Edit each clip down to five to ten minutes and hold a viewing party.

My Soul Has Got to Move

At Horeb, the LORD our God told us:
You've been at this mountain long enough.
—Deuteronomy 1:6

Read Deuteronomy 1:1–8

In a written report of the laws and events after the Exodus, Moses recounts what took place in the forty years of wilderness wanderings. The disobedient generation that worshiped the golden calf in the desert, wanted to return to Egypt, rejected Moses' leadership, and complained about food and shelter had died. It was time to leave the comfort of Mount Horeb and move into the land God had prepared for them. It was time to organize and begin a new life. It was time to possess the land. The covenant made with the ancestors was still in place.

From the disembarking of seventeen black men and three black women from the slave ship on August 20, 1619, at Jamestown, Virginia, until the late twentieth century, there was a widespread migration of Blacks from the rural South to the North and West. During the enslaved period of this country, the North was the "Promised Land." Immediately following the end of the Civil War substantial numbers of freed Blacks began to walk, run, and ride to new lands, seeking better lives and trying to escape racism. They were, however, segregated into ghettos and found a different type of racism in the new land. Even members of the black establishment often viewed them as "country." From 1916 to 1970, during this Great Migration, it is estimated that some six million black Southerners relocated to urban areas in the North and West. The beginning of the twenty-first century began a reverse migration from North to South.

The children of Israel were promised a land flowing with milk and honey, a land of plenty, and a land that they owned as God's chosen people. They did not take the land without a struggle. Many died in the move. Many others died as they were driven from the land. Still others gave up and returned to enslavement of one type or another. Ultimately the land was secured. Blacks in the Great Migration learned that lesson as their descendants learn daily. The promise comes with a cost. Are we willing to pay it?

Prayer: The Promised Land is within our reach. Dear Lord, direct us as we leave our comfort and complacency and begin a journey toward possibility. Amen.

Do: Construct a family migration chart. If you created genealogical archives in an earlier session, if may be helpful to consult them. Discuss all the places three to four generations of your family has lived. Discuss the various cultural, social, economic, spiritual, and personal factors reasons for residing in those places and spaces.

Discuss: In a time of global political unrest, another mass migration of sorts is underway. How can you faithfully respond to the refugee crisis around the world?

Dig Deeper: Develop either your migration chart or family tree further using family records, global positioning system software, digital aids, topographical maps, or globes. Draw a fuller picture of your family's history.

Standing in the Gap

If you have raced with people and are worn out,
   how will you compete with horses?
If you fall down in an open field,
   how will you survive in the forest along the Jordan?
—Jeremiah 12:5

Read Jeremiah 12:1–5

The life of a prophet is not easy. Prophets are called by God to be witnesses before the people. Prophets are called to denunciate. They boldly state that the present situations are not pleasing to God. Prophets annunciate. They express future possibilities in the lives of the people. Prophets speak and act. Prophets stand in the gap for the people and intercede with God. This was the job of Jeremiah, the weeping prophet. His family and friends turned against him, yet he had to continue to minister to them. He often complained to God. Life was too hard. God listened to Jeremiah's whining and patiently told him that life is hard, but it can always become more difficult. He asked the prophet, "If you are having problems with little things in the normal flow of life, what will you do with big problems, sickness, job loss, relationship problems? If you are having problems standing for me when people say they do not like you, what will you do when they say they hate you, treating you like you are nothing?" How can we ever work through tragedy if we faint at the first sign of trouble? If we are unable to stand the pressure of day-to-day occurrences, what happens when some seek to kill us or we face death?

The Buffalo Soldiers dispatched to the Western frontier from 1867 to 1896 must have felt like Jeremiah. These African American cavalry regiments were originally part of the 10th Cavalry at Fort Leavenworth, Kansas. Their principal mission was to control the Indians of the Plains and Southwest. They did not receive the respect afforded other soldiers. They were given aged horses, deteriorating equipment, and inadequate supplies of ammunition. They escorted stagecoaches, trains, and work parties, and policed cattle rustlers and illegal traders. They received little or no honor but stood in the gap for the people anyway.

Prayer: God who calls us from our mother's womb, lead us to stand in the gap even when we do not feel appreciated. Amen.

Do: Prophets speak truth to power. What truth do you need to speak? Using the form of a letter to the editor, write the truth you think today's powers need to hear.

Discuss: Who has put their own safety on the line for you? Who stands in the gap for you?

Dig Deeper: Have you ever wondered about the people who sacrificed their lives and livelihood in places like Korea, Vietnam, Iraq, or Afghanistan so you could live in relative freedom? Visit a local VFW or Wounded Warriors Service to listen to, talk with, or simply thank Black veterans. Watch movies about the Tuskegee Airmen, like Anthony Hemmingway's Red Tails.

On Eagles' Wings

But those who hope in the LORD
*   will renew their strength;*
*   they will fly up on wings like eagles;*
*   they will run and not be tired;*
*   they will walk and not be weary.*
—Isaiah 40:31

Read Isaiah 40:21–31

The psalmist writes that "those who hope in the LORD...will fly up on wings like eagles." The sense of soaring above all the stuff of the world and experiencing the joyous release from restrictions can be exhilarating. Elizabeth "Bessie" Coleman or "Queen Bess" as she was called in the press (1893–1926) was the first black woman to receive a pilot's license and the first woman to get an international pilot's license. She believed she could fly. "Brave Bessie" endured a difficult childhood and a seemingly hopeless young adulthood as a laundress and manicurist until flying captured her imagination. Her childhood dream was to "amount to something." She was a barnstormer or pilot who specialized in parachuting and stunt flying at air shows across the United States. Her tenacity was her hallmark.

Second Isaiah contains an oracle or prophecy about exiled Israelites returning from Babylonian captivity without any obstructions. Mountains will be leveled. Valleys will be elevated. God will comfort the people. The people will recognize God's sovereignty and majesty. Enemies of Israel will be punished. Idols will be exposed as worthless. God will be fully in control and allow those who wait patiently for release to fly like eagles. They reach great heights. They have intractable endurance. They can see vistas that others ignore. They engage life without fear of failure. They are undefeatable. They believe they can fly. They realize that God is carrying them, guiding them, protecting them, and encouraging them along the journey.

Prayer: God of the wind and sky, like an eagle teaches her young to fly, guide me out of my fear of failure and lift me to new heights. Amen.

Do: Write your dreams on a piece of paper. Make a paper airplane and fly it, saying a prayer that God will help you achieve your dreams.

Discuss: If you could do anything and had no chance of failing, what would you do?

Dig Deeper: Black women have been airline pilots, flight engineers, fighter pilots, and astronauts. Have a family "Take Flight Night" and review the life of Bessie Coleman; watch Hidden Figures *(directed by Theodore Melfi); listen to interviews of airline pilots Jill Brown Hiltz, Stephanie Johnson, or Dawn Cook; or research and report on astronauts Mae Jemison, Stephanie Wilson, Joan Higginbotham, and Yvonne Cagle or fighter pilot Shawna Kimbrell.*

The Will to Learn

Teach the wise, and they will become wiser;
  inform the righteous, and their learning will increase.
—*Proverbs 9:9*

Read Deuteronomy 6:4–9

A proverb is a short saying used to educate about basic life truths. In African American culture it is sometimes called "Mother Wit." The Book of Proverbs is a listing of King Solomon's wisdom musings, warnings, and instructions. Proverbs 9:9 is in a section of Proverbs termed "Wisdom's Feast." Wisdom is equated to a gourmet meal that feeds the soul as well as the body. Blacks in the United States were forbidden by law to read and write. Perhaps someone interpreted this proverb as meaning that if Blacks were educated, they would become even wiser than they were. Some persons came to the United States well-educated but due to language and cultural differences were thought to be ignorant. Some had to pretend to be unlettered to survive death or lynching. Perhaps someone believed if Blacks were educated, they would learn how to throw off the shackles of oppression. Perhaps someone thought that if Blacks gained wisdom, they would be on equal footing with their oppressors.

Countless Blacks were killed or abused for trying to read the Bible. Many Whites were sanctioned for teaching Blacks. Still Blacks sought to be educated. Prince Hall and Blacks in Boston petitioned for equal school facilities in 1787. Blacks educated themselves in homes, churches, and schools founded after the Civil War with inferior classrooms and inadequate supplies. In 1955 the United States Supreme

Court wrote an opinion that schools would be integrated "with all deliberate speed." Nine Black students, Ernest Green, Melba Pattillo Minnijean Brown, Elizabeth Eckford, Thelma Mothershed, Gloria Ray, Carlotta Walls, Terrence Roberts, and Jefferson Thomas, were escorted by the 101st Airborne Division to attend Central High School in Little Rock, Arkansas. Four of them eventually graduated. They endured all kinds of hatred to obtain wisdom and knowledge. Their heroic actions opened the door for Blacks to study at most schools in America. Not until October 1969 did the Supreme Court order school segregation "at once" to end.

Prayer: God of wisdom and knowledge, we want to learn more about you. Teach us to become living witnesses of your power. Amen.

Do: Proverbs, Mother Wit, and community sayings are generally dismissed as "that old stuff" when we are younger but take on new meaning as we mature. Comprise a list of "Ten Things My Mother/ Father Used to Say" that you now understand and/or that you find yourself saying to your children or students. Are there some you are still trying to figure out?

Discuss: What is one life lesson you want to pass on? Why did you choose the one you chose?

Dig Deeper: Create a "Family Sayings" poster. Hang it in a central location and allow any family member to add to the list as they notice new or additional sayings.

Anonymous Greatest

Those who humble themselves like this little child
will be the greatest in the kingdom of heaven.
—Matthew 18:4

Read Matthew 18:1–5

Humility has been defined as a lack of pride, meekness, or a sense of submission. Contemporary culture at times treats humility as a weakness. It seems that we are encouraged to be the greatest or most important person in the room, the celebrity, the star, the center of the universe. In the gospel as attributed to Matthew, Jesus is delivering his fourth teaching discourse. In the Roman Empire greatness was associated with wealth, connections, status, and power. The disciples ask Jesus' opinion about who is the greatest person in the community. Jesus, fully aware of societal standards, confounds them by saying one can only be great when she becomes childlike. *Childlike* does not mean childish. Childlike qualities include innocence, simplicity, humility, and courtesy. Being childlike can also mean unabashed bravery, dangerous vulnerability, and insatiable hunger. Disciples, children and adults, need a measure of all of these diverse qualities in order to survive and thrive in the world.

Six-year-old Ruby Bridges exemplifies the greatness Jesus described. This diminutive disciple, immortalized by Norman Rockwell, wanted to go to first grade during the tumultuous 1960 integration wars. A federal court ordered the desegregation of schools in the South. Ruby's father did not want her to go to the school, but her mother insisted. Ruby was enrolled in William Frantz Elementary School in New Orleans. She was the first and only black child at the all-white school. She was escorted to class by U.S. Marshals as adults called her names, threatened to kill her, and spat at her. They withdrew their children from the school, making Ruby the only student in attendance that year. She never missed a day. She was taunted each morning. She never cried. Her family suffered bigotry, loss of jobs, and loss of land; but she completed the school year. In a world where the accomplishments of adults are termed routinely the "greatest," Ruby Bridges and all the other children of the movement were exemplars of true greatness.

Prayer: God who sees all, we thank you for all those persons who continue to do great things even when no one recognizes them. Amen.

Do: Consider who in your family, church, neighborhood or larger community continually does a seemingly small act that impacts many people or who consistently gives of themselves without recognition. Who are the persons in hotels, restaurants, reception areas, parking lots, housekeeping who make life easier for us but are often overlooked? Create a family plan of how to show gratitude or give little acts of human kindness to toward the anonymous among us.

Discuss: How do you define greatness?

Dig Deeper: Read The Story of Ruby Bridges, *written by Robert Coles and illustrated by George Ford. Are there children in your life with whom you can share this story?*

Liberty and Justice for All

There is neither Jew nor Greek; there is neither slave nor free;
nor is there male and female, for you are all one in Christ Jesus.
—Galatians 3:28

Read Galatians 3:25–29

The Declaration of Independence, drafted by Thomas Jefferson between June 11 and June 28, 1776, symbolizes the foundational governing principles of the United States:

> We hold these truths to be self-evident, that all men are
> created equal, that they are endowed by their Creator with
> certain unalienable Rights, that among these are Life,
> Liberty and the pursuit of Happiness.

The history of the United States, however, reflects varied interpretations of the text. The reality has been, and is, that there are persons who do not fully experience these liberties due to their race, gender, sexuality, ethnicity, language, or politics. Bayard Rustin, the chief organizer of the August 23, 1963, March on Washington, lived in shadowed obscurity behind A. Philip Randolph, Martin Luther King, Jr., Rosa Parks, Jesse Jackson, and other leaders of the modern Civil Rights Movement. His philosophy was that God is in every person, loves every person, and promises each person a right to a decent life. Rustin exemplified the principles of the Declaration of Independence but never fully experienced them. He cofounded the Fellowship for Reconciliation and the Congress of Racial Equality. He understood that God's promise of liberty and justice for all was an obtainable mandate.

Paul writes to the church at Galatia about receiving the covenantal promise God made with Abraham. He tells them that through Christ's sacrifice they are not under the law but under grace. There were people who believed that the Galatians did not deserve to be heirs to God's promise. They had forgotten that Abraham received the promise before the law was written. No ethnic separatism, no racial bias, no gender oppression, no age discrimination, and no political privilege stops God's promise.

Prayer: God who loves us all, take away our prejudices so that we can see you in one another and love regardless of who we think others are. Amen.

Do: Sketch out a family or group covenant. What are the responsibilities of each family member toward the others? How are people rewarded or how do they face consequences of upholding or breaking the agreement? How do you know if you are keeping the family promise? If you are not in a group, begin writing a "Rule of Life," which is a kind of patterned and intentional practice of spiritual disciplines, such as prayer, scripture reading, and worship. It is a covenant between you and God that outlines how you will nurture and live out your spiritual life.

Discuss: Galatians wanted to keep divisions, insiders and outsiders. How else do we keep others out of the circle of grace?

Dig Deeper: Flesh out and finalize your family/group covenant or your personal Rule of Life. Are you ready to commit to God and to one another that you will keep this covenant? If so, sign it and post it in a prominent place to remind you of how you agreed to live day by day.

Cast the Vision

There is still a vision for the appointed time;
it testifies to the end;
    it does not deceive.
  If it delays, wait for it;
    for it is surely coming; it will not be late.
—Habakkuk 2:3

Read Habakkuk 2:1–5

During the 1950s Black teachers were respected members of the black middle class. Teachers were esteemed with doctors, lawyers, and preachers. Teaching, primarily in elementary and secondary schools, was one of the few "white collar" professions open to black women. The classroom provided a panoramic view of the world outside of ghettos, farms, and segregated communities. Using second- and third-hand books, black teachers engaged potential writers, scientists, politicians, carpenters, leaders, ministers, domestics, musicians, and educators with precious facts, figures, and life lessons. Educators like Jo Ann Robinson of Montgomery, Alabama, kept the vision of a better life for her students. She knew that change involves risk. She believed in 1955 as that change was about to take place.

The prophet Habakkuk speaks of change in the midst of seemingly hopeless situations. The violent Babylonians were threatening Judah. Habakkuk asks God how long God will allow this persecution. God did not give a strategic timeline, just assurance that the end of oppression would come. Habakkuk was told to stand watch and wait for God's fulfillment.

The stories of the women of the Civil Rights Movement are rarely told. Jo Ann Robinson, an educator and a civil rights activist, was a behind-the-scenes leader of the Montgomery Bus Boycott. She was the president of the Women's Political Council (WPC), which challenged Montgomery's policy of segregated seating on public transportation. She persuaded Ralph Abernathy, Edgar Nixon, and Bayard Rustin to become involved in the boycott. She laid the foundation for the boycott by printing and distributing flyers, organizing mass meetings, and planning the bus boycott. She endured numerous threats and lost her job, but the vision was fulfilled.

Prayer: Activate our imaginations, O Lord. Teach us to wait on you to fulfill our dreams. Amen.

Do: Habakkuk 2:2 reads, "Write the vision, and it make it plain." Writing a vision is an act of faith and commitment. Take a few minutes to consider where you see yourself in five, ten, fifteen, or twenty years. Write your visions down and share them with the group.

Discuss: The Ghanaian principle of "Sankofa" means "to go back and fetch." is the practice of remembering where you been so that you can move forward. Consider how any life lessons you have learned have impacted your present situation. From what do you have yet to learn?

Dig Deeper: After further discussion about your visions, place the pages in a safe or time capsule. At a predetermined time open the capsule/safe and discuss again your life lessons, achievements, need to re-envision, and hopes for the future.

Something Within

But we have this treasure in clay pots
so that the awesome power belongs to God and doesn't come from us.
—2 Corinthians 4:7

Read 2 Corinthians 4:7–10

I am always fascinated by stereotypic critiques of youth. It is as if adults believe they have a market on values, responsibility, intelligence, activism, or faith. Yes, there are some youth who seem to have established permanent residence in discord. Yes, there are some disrespectful young people who thrive on a sense of entitlement. What about those persons who inherently seek to better humanity regardless of what peers or parents are doing?

Trained in the nonviolent protest strategies of Mahatma Ghandi, James Lawson, and Martin Luther King Jr., four black college students—David Richmond, Franklin McCain, Ezell Blair Jr. (Jibreel Khazan), and Joseph McNeil—refused to leave the whites-only counter at the F. W. Woolworth store in Greensboro, North Carolina. This February 1, 1960, sit-in inspired spontaneous national protests at any place with a whites-only policy. The Woolworth sit-in lasted several weeks as other young men and women joined them. Eventually Woolworth's changed its policy of following the local customs on race. Something inside of the young people enabled them to sit in silence for hours, to take the brunt of verbal and physical assault and not respond in kind.

Paul's Second Letter to the Corinthians reads like a ministerial training manual. Challenged on several sides about the veracity of his ministry, Paul tells the church that the believers are fragile, earthen vessels. Our bodies are transitory, but our souls and spirits are precious. There will be hardships in each person's life. The joy is that God has placed a special treasure, an endurance gene, deep down inside of each of us. Just when we think we cannot go any further, God reminds us that resilience, a "Yes, I can," is at our core. That's what the lunch-counter youth discovered. As the old song goes, "Something within I cannot explain; . . . all I know there is something within."

Prayer: Still my heart, O God. Calm my fears, Lord Jesus. Protect me from hurtful words and painful mental and physical assaults. Give me a strong resolve to live past the present moment. Amen.

Do: Using clay or play dough create a small cup or vessel. On a slip of paper, write down your wildest dream or something you currently think is impossible. Place the paper inside your creation and seal it. Place it someplace you pass every day and think about what it would take for you to achieve your dream. How much you are willing or able to risk to make dreams a reality? Open only when you think you have reached your goal. Describe how God made a way for you to achieve your heart's desire.

Discuss: How would you define courage?

Dig Deeper: Cultivate a breath prayer to repeat in difficult moments or times of great fear. A simple breath prayer has two phrases, the first addressing God and the second making a request. Slowly breathe in as you pray the first part of the prayer and breathe out on the second phrase. Repeat multiple times. An example might be, "Loving God, be my strength."

Control Your Own Future

"I can't walk in this," David told Saul,
"because I've never tried it before." So he took them off.
—1 Samuel 17:39b

Read 1 Samuel 17:38–40

The story of David and Goliath found in First Samuel has been recited in Sunday school classes, sermons, children's literature, and even borrowed for secular morality plays. We know that David used a sling and stones to defeat the gargantuan Goliath when others ran and hid. Prior to the encounter, David had a discussion with King Saul about what to wear in battle. Saul offered David the king's armor to protect David against Goliath's sword. David tried on the king's helmet, coat of mail, sword, and armor. David tried to walk but could not move. He took them off and put on his own clothes, and he won the battle.

Archbishop David George Augustus Stallings Jr., grew up in the Roman Catholic Church. He was trained as a priest. He was, however, constantly at odds with the hierarchy, feeling his heritage was never addressed or affirmed. No matter how hard he tried to interest the establishment in Black heritage, he was rebuffed. In 1989, he decided he no longer fit the Catholic Church yet wanted to continue to be a priest. Aware of his violation of church law, Stallings established the Imani Temple African American Catholic Congregation. He celebrated the first mass at the Howard University Law School Chapel on July 2, drawing about two thousand congregants. The worship service was decidedly Afrocentric in liturgy, sermon, and music. Stallings believed that one's spiritual maturity is directly tied to one's cultural affirmation. He was excommunicated from the Roman Catholic Church in 1990.

King David and Archbishop David each realized he had to wear his own clothes. They had to be the persons God created them to be. Both took on Goliaths and in their own way won part of the battle. Each of us must be ourselves, not a clone, not a caricature, not a characterization of someone else. We control our destiny. Will we live it through someone else or walk in our own identity?

Prayer: In the face of life's Goliaths, Lord, enable me to wear my own armor, use my own gifts, and control my own future. Amen.

Do: Take turns pretending to be someone else by dressing up and/or acting like them. Consider what it takes to be that person. Why did you choose that person? What are his or her gifts and graces? What about their difficulties and deficiencies? Take a selfie. Repeat the exercise being yourself. Take another selfie. How does it feel different to be yourself?

Discuss: What do you value about yourself? Do certain traits, characteristics, talents, experiences, and/or skills come to mind? What can you do today to honor the person God created you to be?

Dig Deeper: We often have many people in our lives telling us what (they think) we should be or do. These messages can be powerful. Write a script of how others want or wanted your life to be. Write a script of how you want your life to be. How can you take charge of your own story?

All Things Are Possible

I can endure all these things through the power
of the one who gives me strength.
—Philippians 4:13

Read Philippians 4:4–13

"I can't." "No one will believe me." "I'm afraid." "I don't have the money." "I'm not smart enough." "I'll lose my job." "They'll kill me." We have all heard or used excuses for inaction. Paul understood the reluctance of people who felt disempowered, ostracized, or just tired. The church at Philippi of Macedonia received a prison letter from Paul addressing their opponents, internal dissension, Christian unity, and sustained faith. Paul understood the importance of their work and wanted to undergird them with moral instruction. Work in the midst of constant opposition can lead to breakdowns in relationships, like that between Euodia and Syntyche, and to excuses for incomplete work. Paul exhorts them to think about true, honest, noble, just, pure, pleasing, commendable, excellent, and worthy things, not the problems. Paul urges them to keep on working no matter what. He uses his own life experiences to tell the Philippians that no matter what happens God will provide what we need to finish the task.

Beaten, shot, cursed, jailed, raped, ignored, laughed at, lynched, and loved, hundreds of black and white college and high school students left their secure lives to play a major role in the 1960–1966 campaign to end segregation in the South. The Student Nonviolent Coordinating Committee (SNCC) was created on the campus of Shaw University in Raleigh, North Carolina. SNCC organized the Freedom

Summer voter registration campaigns and worked with the Mississippi Council of Federated Organizations, which included the Congress of Racial Equality (CORE), and the National Association for the Advancement of Colored People (NAACP). Diane Nash, Robert Moses, Marion Barry, John Lewis, Julian Bond, Praithia Hall, Cordell Reagon, Bernice Johnson, Charles Neblett, Stokely Carmicheal, Ella Baker, and Fannie Lou Hamer were just a few of the young people whose "jail no bail" strategy, risked themselves so that the people of Mississippi in particular could vote. God in and around them, they believed they could do all things.

Prayer: God of Possibility, please walk with me. Amen.

Do: What do you want to know about the in-person experience of civil rights activists such as members of SNCC, Black Panthers, SCLC, or local Black Lives Matter members? Formulate a list of questions. Why did/do they protest, and what are their hopes and dreams for our society? If possible, follow up with actual interviews.

Discuss: What excuses do we come up with to "stay out of it"? How can you address one of these excuses?

Dig Deeper: Watch the PBS special documentary series Eyes on the Prize. *After each episode, discuss the people and issues depicted.*

Wake Up, Everybody

Wake up and strengthen whatever you have left,
teetering on the brink of death,
for I've found that your works are far from complete
in the eyes of my God.
—Revelation 3:2

Read Revelation 3:1–6

Harold Melvin and the Blue Notes crooned, "Wake up everybody; no more sleepin' in bed, no more backward thinkin', time for thinkin' ahead."* These lyrics mirror John's message for the church at Sardis. Sardis had a reputation for being alive, but spiritually dead. John tells the people that God is not pleased with their actions and inaction. The good news is that there was time to change their ways. God recognized that there were people in Sardis who followed God's commandments. Finally, John says that if the people wake up and change their ways, God will forgive them, and blot out their sins.

The United States was touted as the land of opportunity, yet institutional slavery was present everywhere. The nation had a veneer of equal prosperity, but a layer of disenfranchisement seethed just beneath it. The rumblings of dissent and revolution began to rock the nation out of its sleep in 1965. The Fifteenth and Nineteenth Amendments to the U.S. Constitution enfranchised black men and women. Southern poll taxes, literacy texts, intimidation, assault, and states laws denied them the right to vote. But the Voting Rights Act of 1965 reinstated the right to vote to Southern Blacks and was to be enforced by the attorney general of the United States. The act was extended for five years in 1970, seven years in 1975, twenty-five years in 1982, and twenty-five more years in 2006. Additionally, federal legislation in 1970 protected voting rights for non–English-speaking citizens. Perhaps the federal government reviewed John's message. Perhaps enough people died trying to gain the vote. Perhaps the character (who we really are) of the country began to overtake its reputation (who others think we are). Perhaps the death knell was too loud. In any event backward thinking was slowly replaced with forward thinking. Perhaps we can still hear John's call today. Recent Supreme Court decisions remind us that the march for voting justice continues on.

Prayer: Shake us into awakening, God. Wipe the sleep from our eyes, enliven our consciousness, and rebuild our character. Amen.

Do: Watch Schoolhouse Rock's *"I'm Just a Bill" to trace the process of how a bill becomes a law.*

Discuss: In what ways do you see the struggle for equal access to the polls as continuing? What can be done about it?

Dig Deeper: Visit local politicians, public service officers, legislatures, and community forums to understand the power of the vote and see how laws affect our daily lives.

*"Wake Up Everybody," written by Carstarphen, Whitehead, and McFadden. © Warner/Chappell Music Inc.

Cardiac Care

Create a clean heart for me, God;
put a new, faithful spirit deep inside me!
—Psalm 51:10

Read Psalm 51

King David was the apple of God's eye. David, the former shepherd boy, was a part of Jesus' human lineage. He was a called, anointed, and appointed leader of God's people. David was poetically and musically talented, handsome, wise, and courageous; yet David did not always do what he was supposed to do. He coveted the wife of another man, ordered him killed, and married his wife, Bathsheba. David's heart, soul, and mind were unhealthy. Psalm 51 is a song or poem requesting forgiveness and pardon for what was done. The author bemoans the fact that he is unable to escape the evidence of his sin. He knows that God is justified in punishing him. He asks God to clean him up, wash away evidence of his crimes, and let him start over with his relationship to God. He requested a clean heart, a redirected life, a new opportunity to be God's chosen one.

David sought spiritual heart surgery, but in 1893 Dr. Daniel Hale Williams performed the first physical open heart surgery. He operated on a stabbing victim, removed the knife from his heart, sutured the sac around his heart; and the man lived for many years. In 1913 Dr. Williams became the only African American in the charter group of the American College of Surgeons. The sac around David's heart, just like our hearts from time to time, was filled with things that were not Godlike: lust, greed, covetousness, lies, pride, jealousy, and murder. He needed open-heart surgery. He asked God to take out his cold stony heart and replace it with a warm fleshy heart of love. The psalmist is not bargaining with God, asking for mercy. He says that after his heart is clean, after the sutures are removed from his mind, after he steps back on the right path, after those he hurt have forgiven him, he will praise God. He will teach others how to live by God's precepts. He will sing about how good God is to him. That is our response after God has cleaned up our hearts and souls.

Prayer: Father of forgiveness, my heart hurts. Please repair it so that I can live as you want me to live. Amen.

Do: Using pencil and paper, draw a heart inside a heart. In the space between the hearts, representing the sac surrounding our hearts, fill in things you need God to remove. Say a prayer asking God to do so, then erase the words and rewrite them outside the hearts.

Discuss: At what points in your life have you, like David, prayed for a fresh start? What happened?

Dig Deeper: Both Meherry Medical College and Morehouse School of Medicine have reputations for educating excellent African American medical professionals. Research the schools' histories and current program offerings.

Time to Dance

You changed my mourning into dancing.
  You took off my funeral clothes
    and dressed me up in joy
—*Psalm 30:11*

Read Psalm 30

Born in 1909, Katherine Dunham grew up like many little Black girls of her generation...poor. Her mother died when she was four. Her father was left to raise two children and was unable to balance fatherhood and finances. As her father traveled, she lived with various relatives until he remarried. She chose to live with a supportive and loving stepmother after that divorce. In college, she became fascinated with dance as a cultural symbol in general and the African Diaspora in particular. Employed in 1938 as choreographer of the Negro Federal Theatre Project, Katherine Dunham devoted her time to family and dance.

The writer of Psalm 30 speaks of dancing in thanksgiving after the recovery from a serious illness, a near-death experience. In the often-quoted verse, "Weeping may stay all night, but by morning, joy!" the faithful know that trouble will not last always (verse 5). Grateful for God's intervention and love in his life, the writer acknowledges God hears and answers prayers. He says that he no longer has to mourn but now can dance joyfully. He trusted God to give him courage for the night seasons.

Katherine Dunham, "Matriarch of Black Dance," learned that God sustained her through all of the night seasons of her youth, the societal roadblocks of her adult life, and even her personal health issues. She let her soul lead her body in expression of emotions and movement to a variety of beats. In the 1940s and 1950s the Dunham School of Dance was the premier facility for African American dancers. She choreographed movies, television, and stage productions like *Cabin in the Sky*. During the latter half of the twentieth century, this trailblazer for the Alvin Ailey American Dance Theater and Arthur Mitchell's Dance Theatre of Harlem, established community dance schools for children.

Prayer: In the beginning you moved over the face of the water, making the waves calmly dance. Thank you, Lord, for moving across days of my life so I can dance to your soul-filling rhythm. Amen.

Do: Have a dance party! Right here, right now!

Discuss: Has dance and movement played a significant role in your development or expression of faith? If yes, how so?

Dig Deeper: Online or in person, watch an African American dance troupe perform.

Supreme Justice

He has told you, human one, what is good and
*   what the LORD requires from you:*
*   to do justice, embrace faithful love,*
*   and walk humbly with your God.*
—*Micah 6:8*

Read Micah 6:6–8

Lawyer, civil rights activist, feminist, poet, biographer, and priest are just a few of Pauli Murray's callings between graduation from Howard University Law School in 1944 and her death in 1985. Like the prophet Micah, Murray lived and died seeking justice for God's people. Micah represented Israel and Judah before God on charges of exploiting God's people, oppression, idolatry, corruption, bigotry, injustice, and covenant violation. Israel understands that it has been unfaithful to God. The leadership petitions God for a sentence reduction. There are suggestions of burnt offerings, dedication of their firstborn, rams, and oil. God informs them that they already knew the answer to the questions. They have to return to what God had always required: do justice, love mercy, and walk humbly with God. The message has not changed in centuries.

Pauli Murray was a cofounder of the Congress of Racial Equality (CORE) in 1942. She worked for the National Urban League, National Association for the Advancement of Colored People (NAACP), National Organization for Women (NOW), the Works Progress Administration, the Workers Defense League, Equality Committee of the American Civil Liberties Union (ACLU), and the 1961 President's

Commission on the Status of Women on Civil and Political Rights. She protested and was jailed at sit-ins and bus rides. She defined her task as actualizing interracial and gender solidarity while fighting Jim and Jane Crow. Murray's quest for justice was unstoppable. In 1976 she entered seminary and was ordained as the first African American woman Episcopal priest in 1977. She practiced justice. She loved mercy. She walked humbly with all her brothers and sisters and before Almighty God.

Prayer: God of justice, you have given us an imperative to live in equality and love. Empower each of us to stand on your word so that all persons may experience your mercy. Amen.

Do: Make a list of ways of how not to treat one another.

Discuss: Who have been the women in your life who have stood up for God's people and fought for justice?

Dig Deeper: Research local African American community organizations, such as a sororities, fraternities, or service organizations. How could you be a part of their work? Pick one. Can you commit to helping them for the next year? How so?

Singing Your Own Song

Shout triumphantly to the LORD, all the earth!
—*Psalm 100:1*

Read Psalm 100

"Everybody ought to praise God!" "I know life is hard, but God has been good to us!" "You're going through trouble right now, but after while you are gonna shout!" "Tell it!" "Shout!" "Dance it out!" "Say a Word!" "Sing it!" These expressions have resounded in black worship services for centuries. Regardless of the situation of one's day-to-day life, come Sunday it is time to tell your neighbor that God is good. In Psalm 100 everyone is called to praise God. One of the ways that Blacks historically expressed their belief that God is always in charge is through gospel music.

Gospel music is decidedly African American in origin. It is an amalgamation of black Christian faith stances, white Protestant lyricism, African percussive rhythms, spiritual endowment, existential black social life, embodiment of the biblical text, call and response, and improvisation. The first gospel music collection, *Gospel Hymns and Sacred Songs* by Philip Bliss was published in 1874. *Gospel Pearls* was published in 1921 by the National Baptist Convention. Charles Albert Tindley (1851–1933), composed nearly fifty hymns, including "Stand By Me," "Nothing Between," and "We'll Understand It Better By and By." Thomas A. Dorsey (1899–1993), the "Father of Gospel Music," composed such standards as "Precious Lord, Take My Hand," and "There Will Be Peace in the Valley." Other gospel music pioneers include Lucy Campbell ("Something Within"), and Herbert Brewster

("Surely God Is Able"), Theodore Frye, Sallie Martin, Kenneth Morris, Clara Ward, Marion Williams, the Gay Sisters, the Soul Stirrers, and the Gospel Harmonettes. James Cleveland (1931–1991), the "Crown Prince of Gospel," composed more than five hundred songs including "Oh, Lord, Stand By Me," "He's Using Me," "Jesus Is the Best Thing That Ever Happened to Me," and "Peace Be Still." Every soloist, quartet, ensemble, choir, arranger, musician, or director understood they had to make a joyful noise to God with every breath they breathed.

Prayer: I want to sing. I need to sing. I may be sweetly melodic. I may be deeply soulful. I may be off key. I may be tone deaf. I have to tell somebody about what you have done for me. Praise the Lord! Amen.

Do: Teach one another your favorite gospel or faith-centered songs. Sing a few!

Discuss: Describe a time in your life, if ever, when you couldn't bring yourself to sing praises to God. What was going on? How did the issue resolve?

Dig Deeper: Hold a spiritual or hymn sing highlighting Black composers at your home or church. Research the origin of songs and their composers. How do the songs speak to current forms of spirituality and society?

God's Servant Leader

The Spirit of the Lord is upon me.
—Luke 4:18

Read Luke 4:16–21

Adam Clayton Powell Jr., was the first African American Congressman from a northeastern state. He served as Harlem, New York's congressman from 1945 until 1971. He was charismatic, controversial, and compelling. He was the pastor of the Abyssinian Baptist Church in Harlem. Powell was the preeminent civil rights leader of his time. His congressional work contributed to the successful passing of "The Great Society," Medicare, Medicaid, Head Start, equal employment, and contributions to the Civil Rights Act of 1964. Powell was a gifted man who, like most of us, was not perfect. He was used by God, however, to help change the world.

Standing in a temple at Nazareth, Jesus launched his three-year ministry by reading from a scroll containing the words of Isaiah. He knew that persons listening did not believe in what he was saying, others would eventually try to kill him, and still others would one day follow his teachings. Jesus states that the Holy Spirit directs and protects the servant. Jesus frames possible service tasks for those who would follow him. People who are confused, depressed, tired, grieving, lost, and faith-filled need to hear good news. People who feel socially, emotionally, physically, and spiritually imprisoned need to be freed. People who have no hope need to see light in their tunnels. People who have been held back by anything or anyone need to be able to live life to the fullest. Everyone needs to know that help is on the way.

Adam Clayton Powell and all the leaders of yesterday, today, and tomorrow know that pubic service does not carry a guarantee of success. The good news is that with the anointing of the Holy Spirit, ordinary people can do extraordinary things. They can be servant leaders even though they themselves are imperfect beings. In all our work, whether voluntary or paid, it is the Spirit of the Lord working through us that allows us to be servant leaders.

Prayer: Use me, Lord, in your service, through the power of your anointing, and not in my own strength. Amen.

Do: The Bible is full of ordinary people who accomplish extraordinary things. Make a list. Draw or describe your favorite.

Discuss: On whom do you see God's anointing for leadership, perhaps even to public service? How can you tell?

Dig Deeper: Organize a service opportunity for your family, group, or congregation. Read with kids at a tutoring center, organize supplies at a food bank, deliver Meals on Wheels, volunteer at a hospital . . . the possibilities are endless.

This Is My Story

*As for us, we can't stop speaking about
what we have seen and heard.*
—Acts 4:20

Read Acts 4:1–22

Luke writes about a diverse community in the Acts of the Apostles. The fourth chapter details Peter and John's trial before a tribunal in Jerusalem. Anna, Caiaphas, John, and Alexander were among the priestly judges hearing the case. Peter and John taught under Solomon's portico about Jesus' life and resurrection. The government was worried and asked who authorized the apostles to teach and work miracles. They had neither been educated by the state nor certified as physicians, yet lives were being changed. Peter and John began to repeat the story of Jesus and the empowerment they received as his followers. They even reminded the high priests that the leaders were the ones who sentenced Jesus to death. The evidence of their healing acts was in court. The man who had lain at the gate of the Temple his entire life and walked away accompanied them. After deliberation in chambers the council's sentence was that Peter and John had to stop talking about what had happened. The apostles, however, replied, "We cannot stop talking about what we know. We have seen and heard too much to keep it to ourselves."

Ernest James Gaines, born in 1933, has a story to tell. He uses his life on a cotton plantation in Louisiana as his source. He is a prolific author of historical novels. His stories are told in first person with an entrancing blend of humor and drama. His works include *The*

Autobiography of Miss Jane Pittman, In My Father's House, A Gathering of Old Men, and *Lesson Before Dying.* Several of his works have been made into movies. In a world where many keep quiet about their experiences, particularly painful memories, Gaines could not keep quiet about what he had seen and heard. He understands that many are healed when they read or see his words. Many recognize that they share experiences with others. Many can sing with the apostles, psalmist, and song writer, "This is my story, this is my song, praising my Savior all the day long."

Prayer: Lord, thank you for all I have seen and heard. Let me boldly share it with others so that your works are known in all the earth. Amen.

Do: Write down five little-known facts about yourself. Compile the lists and take turns guessing who said what.

Discuss: If you were writing an autobiography, what would name the chapters? What parts of your life are most significant for you to highlight?

Dig Deeper: Select age-appropriate biographies or autobiographies of African Americans often overlooked during Black History Month and other celebrations. Meet again to share what you learned.

That's Love

*If I speak in tongues of human beings and of angels
but I don't have love, I'm a clanging gong or a clashing cymbal.*
—1 Corinthians 13:1

Read 1 Corinthians 13

This passage of Paul's first letter to the church at Corinth follows an explanation of spiritual gifts and is followed by an exhortation on gifts of prophecy and speaking in tongues. Paul teaches that one is not given gifts for the sake of being better than anyone else but for the good of the entire community. Chapter 13 is used in many wedding ceremonies to symbolize the type of love wives and husbands should possess, love that is patient, kind, unselfish, sensitive, humble, joyful, forgiving, strong, enduring, and supportive. This is *agape* love, the love that embraces in spite of who we are or what we have done. Chapter 13 says that godly love is eternal while other spiritual gifts will end. This type of love comes only through faith in God, in obedience to God's commands, by God's Spirit, for all of God's people. If we do not exhibit this type of love, we are making a lot of noise but saying nothing.

In the mid-1970s, I was teaching at a small Missouri college and had the opportunity to meet a man who exemplified agape love, Ossie Davis. He and his wife traveled for hours in a storm to speak with about two hundred black students during a Black History celebration. He never complained about the size of the crowd, the homey atmosphere, the star-struck responses, or the lack of press coverage. He was focused on sharing his vision of justice and equality in America and reminding us of our responsibility to remember our heritage. He was humble, loving, almost grandfatherly, and made each student feel important. When he spoke, wisdom and passion seemed to flow from every pore. Davis was a writer, director, actor, playwright, producer, and a strong voice for artists' rights, human dignity, and social justice. He joined crusades for jobs and freedom and helped raise money for the Freedom Riders. He eulogized both Martin Luther King and Malcolm X. He used his voice to connect the community, to raise the consciousness of humanity, and to love each person in spite of who they were or where he found them.

Prayer: Jesus, guide my tongue so that I speak only love. Amen.

Do: Read aloud Corinthians 13, substituting your name for "love." Do you live up to those values? Write the paraphrased chapter and post it as inspiration to grow in love.

Discuss: In what areas of life is it hardest to embrace agape love? What's one thing you can do or say to move toward a more all-encompassing love in that situation or relationship?

Dig Deeper: View theater productions or digital editions of plays by Black authors, such as Davis' Pearlie Victorious.

I Will Survive

I won't die—no, I will live
  and declare what the LORD has done.
—Psalm 118:17

Read Psalm 118:11–17

God saves us on purpose. God has a plan for each life. There are times when it seems like we teeter on the brink of death, yet God, in the words of the ancestors, causes "our golden moments to roll on." I believe that God has anointed doctors to be intercessors in our life-and-death struggles. When we sense our bodies are out of sync, many seek medical assistance. African Americans have an extensive history of herbal or alternative medicine, home remedies, preventative cleansings, spiritual cures, and formal medical training.

Doctor Lucas Santomee (1660s) was the first university-trained black physician. In 1787, Doctor John Derham became the first black medical doctor in America. Dr. James McCune Smith (1811–1865) treated black and white patients, and countered racist beliefs that Blacks were mentally inferior to whites. Doctor Rebecca Lee Crumpler (1864) was the first black American-educated doctor. For fifty years the only black physician in Colorado was Dr. Justina Ford (1871–1952). She reportedly delivered more than seven thousand babies. Doctor Ben Carson Sr. is a world-renowned pediatric neurosurgeon who at one time performed more than five hundred surgeries per year. Each doctor shared the gift of healing with countless people. Each overcame personal obstacles, yet validated the words of the psalmist.

Psalm 118 is a victory song. It begins by giving thanks to God for everlasting goodness. The psalmist sings of God's deliverance of all faithful people. Lives were in peril, but God rescued. God lifted the falling. God strengthened the weak. The psalmist boldly states that regardless of the situation, he will not die but will live to tell others of God's goodness. When a body is sick, the pain at times blocks our view of God. When we are in the midst of healing, we have glimpses of what life can be. When we are healed, we can sing the victory song in full voice.

Prayer: Creator of every fiber of my being, I am thankful that you have saved me to help save others. Amen.

Do: Do a two-minute body scan. Starting at the top of your head, slowly and quietly move your focus down through your body. What feelings and sensations do you notice? Is your body telling you something?

Discuss: When you have been in physical pain, how has it affected your faith and/or your ability and willingness to praise God?

Dig Deeper: Invite a black doctor to present on a public health topic, such as heart disease, diabetes, or obesity.

You Can't Teach What You Don't Know

Make an effort to present yourself to God as a tried-and-true worker, who doesn't need to be ashamed but is one who interprets the message of truth correctly.
—2 Timothy 2:15

Read 2 Timothy 2:14–26

As a child of the fifties, I was taught that education was a ticket out of despair. I immersed myself in books and took mental trips to every country in the world, gained appreciation for ancient cultures, and developed a love of language. In my young adult life I was told, "You can't teach what you don't know, and you can't lead where you won't go." In church my entire life I have heard about studying to show one's self approved."

In the biblical texts, Jesus' disciples study and learn as well as teach. They sat in Jesus' classes and learned about the kingdom of heaven, how to live with one another, and God's commandments. They were then dispatched to teach others. Good teachers are first good students. Good teachers never stop learning. The passage in Second Timothy blatantly rejects false teaching and disreputable teachers. Teachers have an obligation to share well-researched, useful, truthful, and edifying information.

I was led to broaden my knowledge and to acquaint myself with the lives of men and women who took this path before me. Alexander Lucius Twilight was the first African American college graduate, receiving a bachelor's degree from Middlebury College in 1823. Mary Jane Patterson was the first African American woman to receive a bachelor's degree in 1862 at Oberlin College. Sadie Tanner Mossell Alexander received her doctorate in economics in 1921 and a Juris Doctorate in 1927. W. E. B DuBois received his bachelor's degree from Fisk in 1888 and was the first black person to earn a Ph.D. from Harvard in 1895. Eva Beatrice Dykes received her doctorate in English philology in 1921. Georgiana Simpson received her doctorate in 1921 in German from the University of Chicago. Anna Julia Cooper was the fourth black woman to receive a doctorate. In 1925 she defended a dissertation from the Sorbonne in Paris, France, in French entitled, "The Attitude of France toward Slavery during the Revolution." None of them had an easy road, but in order to lead they had to learn.

Prayer: Teach me, Master. Open my mind so I can teach others. Amen.

Do: Pick one teacher who impacted your life. Write him or her a thank-you note. If possible, mail or e-mail it to them. Teachers can't be thanked enough!

Discuss: Who have been the most influential teachers in your life, both formal or informal, in school and out of school?

Dig Deeper: Research Historically Black Colleges and Universities (HBCUs). Pay attention to each school's purpose, founders, origin, early and current faculty and administration, activism, alumni, and scholarship. Take a visit if possible.

Can You Imagine?

Faith is the reality of what we hope for,
the proof of what we don't see.
—Hebrews 11:1

Read Hebrews 11

Otis Boykin (1920–1982) patented the electrical resistor on February 21, 1961. He is responsible for inventing the electrical device used in all guided missiles and computers, twenty-six other electronic devices, and a control unit for heart pacemakers. Mark Dean (1957–) led the team that built a gigahertz computer chip in 1999. Philip Emeagwali (1954–) designed the fastest computer on earth in 1989, "The Connection Machine." In every generation there are persons who are gifted with seeing the invisible, expecting the impossible, and achieving the incredible. They always seem to anticipate a breakthrough. They believe something will happen even when others say there is no way it can take place. Their curiosity is unquenchable. They are ever hopeful. They have almost an extrasensory trust that a discovery is just about to be birthed. Can you imagine?

In what has been called the "Faith Hall of Fame," the writer of Hebrews lists brief biographical sketches of historical exemplars of belief in the unimaginable. Each person overcame doubt, fear, confrontations, loneliness, or enemies by a conviction that anything and everything is possible with God's help. Some left home not knowing what was ahead of them. Some were tested to the limit of their intelligence and emotion. Some died without seeing the fruition of their actions. All came to know a miracle-working God who never lied or left them.

Each pleased God by his or her faithfulness and received a reward. Can you imagine the realization of your wildest dreams? Can you imagine being in a different place tomorrow than you are today? Can you imagine discovering a cure to a disease, saving a nation, or loving an enemy? Can you imagine?

Prayer: Paint my imagination, Lord. Open my ears. Stimulate my mind. Let me never doubt that all things are possible if I can believe. Amen.

Do: What can you dream for God's kingdom? Make a preferred future map: On one edge of a piece of paper, describe where you are today. On the opposite edge, describe where you would like to be at some designated point in the future. In between, line out the steps you need to take to reach your preferred future.

Discuss: If you have no restraints, what could and would you do for God and God's people?

Dig Deeper: Hold a family or group testimony service allowing time for each person to share how good God has been to them. End with singing "I Need You to Survive" or "We Shall Overcome."

Speak for Yourself

Once you weren't a people,
but now you are God's people.
—1 Peter 2:10

Read 1 Peter 2:1–10

Out of the shadows of minstrel shows, black face, derogatory images, and Black-life caricatures emerged actor James Hewlett and the first black theater troupe, the New York-based African Company in 1821–1823. Into the marvelous light of realistic portrayals of Black life came actress Anita Bush, who organized the Anita Bush Players, the first major Black professional company in 1915. *Three Plays for a Negro Theater* by playwright Ridgely Torrence opened at the Garden Theatre in New York City on April 5, 1917. Robert Hooks, Douglas Turner Ward, and Gerald Krone formed the Negro Ensemble Company in 1967. This was followed by an explosion of Black theatre in the 1960s by Amiri Baraka (*Dutchman*), Lorraine Hansberry (*A Raisin in the Sun*), Langston Hughes (*Tambourines to Glory*), and Zora Neale Hurston (*Mule Bone*). Since the 1980s Black theater has been dominated by the works of the domain of August Wilson's *Fences*; *Joe Turner's Come and Gone,* with Langston Hughes' *The Piano Lesson, Jitney*, and *Ma Rainey's Black Bottom*. God's people had to find vehicles to speak of their own culture and ways of being. No one can tell your story like you can tell it. These artists truthfully claimed their humanity. They performed plays in which Blacks were more than one-dimensional uneducated domestics. Their characters were multifaceted human beings, God's people.

Peter writes that we are to approach God's throne as living stones. Many will reject us just as they rejected Jesus. We are to sacrificially prepare ourselves to be part of God's spiritual house. We must purge ourselves of anything that is not godly—malice, insincerity, envy, and slander. We must remove our masks and make-up of pretense, and become who we are destined to be. We are God's children, God's creation, God's people. Others may say we are nobodies, but by God's mercy we are somebodies. We do not have to be understudies for anyone. We are required to proclaim to all the world by thought, word, deed, song, sermon, prayer, character, and witness. We are to remember that God has called us out of the shadows, off the sidelines, from the back into the light, the center, and the forefront of life.

Prayer: God who designed the stages of our life, thank you for calling us from the wings into center stage. Let us perform our parts with vigor and never succumb to acting like others. Amen.

Do: In whatever medium you prefer (words, visuals, music, movement, etc) describe the masks you wear every day. What would it take to drop the mask and let you *show through?*

Discuss: How have you let other people speak for you? What can you do to speak for yourself?

Dig Deeper: Invite African American pastoral counselors or psychologists to present ways to effectively work thought emotional and spiritual difficulties encountered based on cultural norms and particularities.